- Self-proclaimed geniuses are stupid. I know this because I am very clever.

- Jehovah's witnesses: improving my hiding skills since 1976.

- Does anyone else remember when apples and blackberries were just fruits?

- Don't be fooled. Bread knives can be used to cut cheese and other things.

- If your parents never had any children chances are I am talking to myself.

- I was going to get my teeth whitened then I though "I'll just get a tan."

- Always remember you are unique. Just like everyone else.

- How do you know it's windy? When you go outside and it's windy.

- People often walk up to me and ask "what are you doing in my garden?"

- What happens if you through a pebble into the North Sea? It gets wet.

- I've still never seen myself blink.

- Laziness is resting before you get tired.

- What does affect your statutory rights?

- You know you have to start acting your age when you still count the number of steps.

- I phoned a call centre and the automatic message told me all their operators were engaged. Congratulations to them all. Now please answer the phone.

- You know you've reached a new low when its' easier to move house than tidy up.

-

- Next time you are in a cubicle in Marks and Spencer's and there are customers waiting, say to them "I'd give it 5 minutes before you in."

- Sometimes I get lonely. Especially when I'm throwing a Frisbee.

- My definition of an intellectual is someone who can listen to the William Tell overture and not think about the Lone Ranger.

- People are always telling me to get fit. I get enough exercise just pushing my luck.

- I asked the librarian to direct me to the spy thriller section. It was very hush-hush.

- The sooner you fall behind the longer you have to catch up.

- Someone who says they are 99.9% sure is not really sure at all.

- There's one thing I can't stand when I'm drunk. Straight.

- I had a night on the tiles last night. I fell asleep on the scrabble board.

- I have taken up rolling my own cigarettes. Has anyone got any tips?

- Support your local search and rescue squad – get lost.

- I've noticed one side of my house is warmer than the other. It is always colder on the outside.

- I prefer skips to quavers. You can't hide a body in a quaver.

- Have I got multiple personalities? A part of me says yes.

- My friend has multiple personalities. They are some of the nicest people I have ever met.

-

- I sang live with 'The Rolling Stones' once. They were on the radio and I was in my car.

- I worked in a pathology lab but got asked to leave after one of my reports said 'Autopsy' as cause of death.

- Here's a joke for all you mind readers out there …

- I haven't made a prediction in my life and I never will.

- You call it lazy; I call it selective participation.

- I like to imagine that complete strangers are in complete awe of my fitness when I run up stairs two at a time.

- I like to stand in front of the toaster and try not to flinch when it pops out.

- I know a lot about cars. I can look at their headlights and know exactly which direction it is coming from.

- I had to laugh to myself this morning. Because I've got no friends.

- I'm such a thrill seeker that every time I see a 'Caution; Wet Floor' sign, I start running.

- I always wanted to be somebody but I should have been more specific.

- People will believe anything if you whisper it to them.

- I have no sense of direction – I'm not really sure where this is going.

- You snooze you lose unless it's a sleeping competition.

- My extra sensitive toothpaste doesn't like it when I use other toothpastes.

- To cut a long story short just read the first and last pages.

-

- Why are all the unpacking instructions on the inside of the box?

- Yawning is the body's way of saying '10% battery remaining'.

- I bought my friend a nice house warming gift. An electric heater.

- Simon says jump. But Simon never said land so you are all out.

- Ive just fitted a new baby seat in my car. I don't have a child but I do want a good parking space at the supermarket.

- An easy way to upset children is to make them scrambled eggs, cover it in tomato sauce and tell them that was Humpty Dumpty.

- No matter how loud car alarms are, the cars never seem to wake up.

-

- I've never seen an invisible person which goes to prove that they do exist.

- If someone becomes addicted to counselling how would you help them?

- I've just heart that the guy who invented Vaseline is up for the Noble prize. He'll be in the non-friction section.

- I bought some lion repellent the other day. Seems to be working quite nicely.

- I think there should be another day named 'Someday' – can you imagine all the great things that would happen on it?

- Sometimes it seems I spend half of my life breathing in.

- I love my six pack which is why I always protect it with several layers of fat.

- Next time you are in a life with some strangers, turn to face them and say "I suppose you are wondering why I gathered you all here today?"

- There are two words in life that will open doors for you. Push and pull.

- What's green and rectangular? An orange in disguise.

- Anyone know where I can find Bill Payer? I need his permission.

- I'm starting to believe I'm physic but then again, I already knew that.

- I've said it before and I'll say it again; there is nothing more irritating than people repeating themselves.

- Reading while sunbathing makes you well red.

- Why is there so much month left at the end of my money?

-

- I don't really want a t-shirt but a FREE tampon? Now you're talking.

- I've never been told I'm a bad listener.

- I'm indecisive. Or am I?

- I really wouldn't be surprised or bothered if I had no emotion.

- I had a psychic chicken – it was always walking to the other side.

- My fake plants died because I forgot to water them.

- You know you're getting older when an all-nighter means not having to get up to go to the bathroom.

- Does anyone else think that reincarnation is making a comeback?

- My agent told me to use a pen name; I'm now known as Bic Parker.

-

- Here is an announcement for people with prominent teeth: brace yourself.

- My favourite kind of maths is adding insult to injury.

- I never apologise. Sorry but that's just the way I am.

- My wife brings me so much joy. Oops typo, I meant wifi.

- You know what's really great about being a narcissist? Me.

- Why is it nobody ever listens to me until I fart?

- Just recorded the first episode of a murder mystery on a plane. It was the pilot.

- I can't stand broken legs.

- Studying: the act of texting, eating and watching TV with an open textbook nearby.

-

- Never play poker with people with OCD – they'll clean up.

- If I was an optician I'd make the shop sign blurry.

- I was browsing the web today and a spider bit me.

- The price of balloons hse gone up – I blame inflation.

- You know it's raining when you go outside and get wet.

- Common sense is like deodorant. Those who need it most never use it.

- Walking past an O2 shop an assistant asked me who my mobile was with. I answered "Me" and kept walking.

- I know you shouldn't text and drive but I've only had 2 – 3 texts so I should be ok.

- I scored 326 with one throw. No can said I couldn't throw a hedgehog.

- I'm a nightmare in the mornings. I like to run around with a mask on waving a knife.

- I swerved to avoid some nails on the road this morning. I couldn't believe it when the police arrested me for tacks evasion.

- When I die I want to be buried with darts and my car keys just to fool archaeologists?

- To get the crease out of your clothes you have to strike while the iron is hot.

Printed in Great Britain
by Amazon